═ MINI ═
Twister

T0364007

RUNNING PRESS
PHILADELPHIA

Running Press
Hachette Book Group
1290 Avenue of the Americas, New York, NY 10104
www.runningpress.com
@Running_Press

First Edition: April 2018

Published by Running Press, an imprint of Perseus Books, LLC, a subsidiary of Hachette Book Group, Inc. The Running Press name and logo is a trademark of the Hachette Book Group.

The publisher is not responsible for websites (or their content) that are not owned by the publisher.

Hand illustrations © Gettyimages.com/Lesia_G

ISBN: 978-0-7624-9171-1

C●NTENTS

INTRODUCTION

A popular pastime for more than 50 years, Twister is a classic game that is loved by fans of all ages. Since its inception, the concept of the game that "ties you up in knots" has inspired a variety of exciting interpretations, with newer iterations including technology and music. Today, the Twister brand continues to offer experiences that entertain families across the globe, the latest being this new mini "twist" on the classic game— now you can play with your fingers! Perfectly portable, this mini version of the original Twister game can be played anywhere and includes a mini Twister mat, spinner, and tube socks for your fingers. We'll get into the rules of Mini Twister, but first let's take a walk through the game's colorful 50-year history with some fun Twister facts.

══ FUN FACT! ══

In 1987, 4,160 students at the University of Massachusetts Amherst positioned hundreds of Twister mats together and set a world record for the largest Twister game ever played.

H●W IT BEGAN

In 1964, Reyn Guyer, the toy inventor who developed Nerf five years later, owned a design company with his father. While he was trying to design a promotion for Johnson Wax's Shoe Polish, he developed an idea for a game that uses people as the playing pieces and a mat on the floor as the game board. He called his first attempt "King's Footsie" and pitched the idea to 3M, where, unfortunately, it was rejected.

Guyer hired two game developers, Charles Foley and Neil Rabens, and set up a design team that created several games based on the players-as-pawns concept. The team rearranged the colored dots in a row on the "King's Footsie" mat, making the players use their hands as well as their feet to become more knotted and renamed the game "Pretzel." Two years later, the team brought "Pretzel" and other mat games to The Milton Bradley Company in Springfield, Massachusetts, where the executives considered the concepts. "Pretzel" was chosen after the executives watched other employees get tangled up while demonstrating it.

The Milton Bradley Company officially changed the game's name to "Twister." The company faced some issues as it was socially unacceptable at that time to be as close to others as Twister required. The Milton Bradley Company was still convinced the Twister game would sell, and scheduled its first appearance at Toy Fair.

That same year, the Milton Bradley Company released the Twister game. It was the first game on store shelves that used players' bodies as playing pieces and required them to bend and stretch in challenging positions. In the game of Twister, each player gives the spinner a whirl to see which colored spot they must place their hands or feet on the mat while maintaining their balance. The last player standing wins!

At first, consumers had difficulty understanding the concept of Twister, and they were not inclined to purchase the game. As a result, Twister was reluctantly pulled off the market, and all of the support advertising was cancelled in early 1966.

Before all hope was lost, fortunately Milton Bradley's

Public Relations Company had scheduled a paid appearance for the Twister game on *The Tonight Show*. On May 3rd in 1966, *The Tonight Show* changed everything. The show's host, Johnny Carson, challenged his guest for that evening to a game of Twister. The audience roared with laughter as they watched the two celebrities stretch their bodies into unusual positions, challenging each other's dexterity.

The Twister game's debut on *The Tonight Show* sent consumers rushing to the stores to buy their own Twister game. Abercrombie & Fitch was the only store left with any Twister games in stock, and it soon became overwhelmed with customers. Eventually, Sears changed their minds and restocked the Twister game.

By early 1967, more than three million Twister games were sold.

═══ FUN FACT! ═══

The Strong National
Museum of Play inducted
Twister into the National
Toy Hall of Fame in 2015
alongside Puppets and
Super Soakers.

VARIATIONS
ON THE
CLASSIC GAME

Due to the popular demand of
the Twister game, the brand has
introduced many exciting product
extensions over the years. In
2003, Hasbro released Twister
Moves, a game that combined
the Twister concept with dance

moves and pop music. In the portable social game, players were challenged by a virtual DJ to follow the dance moves and match their feet to a color-coded mat. In 2006, the Twister Dance DVD took dancing and music even further. Players followed step-by-step instructions from a TV-based dance coach who demonstrated 40 different dance moves set to music.

In 2007, Hasbro took the fun outdoors with an exciting Twister line that encouraged free form play (running, jumping, ducking, and dodging) for the entire family. These games included Twister Scram, Twister Take Out, and Twister Dodgeball. Other Twister games that have been released in more recent years include Twister Hopscotch and Twister Hoopla. With the Twister Hopscotch game, children could play hop-scotch year-round with an indoor non-slip mat, and Twister Hoopla "twisted" the classic game even further with players becoming the Twister mat, and the iconic dots turning into rings.

And now comes the latest iteration for Twister fans—a new miniature version that you can play with your fingers: Mini Twister!

In 2015, singer Thomas Rhett and his fans took part in a huge Twister game on the world record breaking Twister mat, which measured 27,159,616 square feet.

H●W T● PLAY
MINI TWISTER

Mini Twister is played the exact same way as traditional Twister; however one big difference is that rather than using their limbs, players utilize their fingers! Also, the original game is often played with more than two players, but for the mini version, just two are

recommended due to the small size (and only two pairs of finger socks are included). Here are the official game rules of this miniaturized version of the classic game:

- Place the mat on a flat surface, and then position both players on opposite sides of the mat, facing each other.

- Designate a third person as the referee. During the game, the referee will spin the spinner, call out the moves, and monitor the game play.
- Each player puts their mini tube socks on their pointer finger and middle finger of the hand in play—one player is red, the other is blue.

- Each player places their pointer finger on the yellow circle and their pinky finger on the blue circle that is closest to their side of the mat.
- The referee spins the spinner, then calls out the finger and the color that the arrow points to. For example, the referee may call out, "Ring finger, red." Both players, at the same time, must then try to

place the called-out finger on a vacant circle of the called-out color. If the referee calls out "Ring finger, red," each player must try to place their ring finger on any vacant red circle.

- If your called-out finger is already on a circle of the called-out color, the player must try to move it to another circle of the same color.

- There can never be more than one finger on any one circle. If the players reach for the same circle, the referee must decide which player got there first. The other player must find another vacant circle of the same color.

- Never remove your finger from a circle unless directed by the referee after a spin. (*Exception*: You may lift a finger to allow another finger to pass by, as long as you announce it to the referee beforehand, and replace the finger on its circle immediately afterward.)

- Any player whose palm touches the mat is immediately out of the game. The last hand left in the game is the winner!

══ FUN FACT! ══

The iconic Twister brand celebrated five decades of right-hand reds in 2016! For the 50th anniversary, Reyn Guyer published a book, *Right Brain Red*, which tells the tale of his creative career and offers the complete story of the Twister game's exciting beginnings.

This book has been bound
using handcraft methods and
Smyth-sewn to ensure durability.

Designed by Ashley Todd.